MW00680517

A Gift for _____

From _____

Why did the chicken _really_ cross the road?

Funny Answers from Famous People - Past & Present

By Mark Millman

Illustrations by Bill Pike

ISBN 0-9769604-0-0

Editing by Margareta Gannon
Book design and main cartoons by Bill Pike
Additional cartoons and flip movie by Robin Olimb
Book production design by Fiona Raven
Business management and marketing by
    Andrew Barden

First Printing July 2005
Printed in the USA

Published by PY Press
1106 Second Street, Suite 324
Encinitas, CA 92024
Tel: 1-866-339-4619
www.jest-a-minute.com

PY PRESS
Sharing the Gift of Laughter

Disclaimer

All of the quotes appearing in this book are entirely fictitious. None of the statements are intended to represent any opinions or actual statements made by any person named. The intention of this book is to spread a little humor and the quotes are designed merely to express the idiosyncratic character of the person and are not meant to be disrespectful to anyone living or dead.

The author, publisher, and any and all persons or entities involved in any way in the preparation, publication, sale, or distribution of this book disclaim all responsibility for the legal effects or consequences of anyone using this book in any way that may defame anyone mentioned in this book. No representations, either express or implied, are made or given regarding the content in this book. Purchasers and persons intending to use this book for any other purpose than private reading are advised that they accept all responsibility for any statements made from the book or representations in any public broadcast.

This book is dedicated to the guiding force
and inspiration in my life, Paramahansa Yogananda,
and to my children, Matthew, Ryan, and Rosina.

Acknowledgements

Naturally, a book needs a lot of help and guidance to get off the ground. All of the people mentioned here have played either a minor or a major role in the process. In order to thank them all and not omit anyone, I will thank them 'in order of appearance,' so to speak. The seed of the idea sprang from some humor that was being shared by my good friend Ranji Rao one evening. From there, Beth Folsom and Brian Kurbejweit added fuel to the fire with their enthusiasm. Once the manuscript was written, it took my mentor and twice- published author, Rhea Atwood, to get me motivated to seek publication. Rhea's determination and encouragement was invaluable. I would also like to thank Doug Glener for his straight forward advice and encouragement.

Thanks also to Margareta Gannon and George Goddard for their proofreading and constructive criticism. Special thanks goes to Joe Granata, John Deters, Rusty Wells, Emmanuel Scaramozzino, Zariah Ricossa and Greg Voisen for believing in the project and getting it off the ground. Above all, I want to thank my wife, Cathy for her undoubting encouragement, valuable editorial contributions and protective influence. A very special thank you to my partner, Andrew Barden, for so many skills, energy and long hard hours working to get the book and web site ready for market, and being a much needed sounding board and contributor of great ideas. This book was a true collaboration by my dear friends. Finally I would like to thank Stan Kegel for all his great work and also the team and contributors at www.WhyDidTheChicken CrossTheRoad.com for allowing us to use some of their quotes.

To all these friends and family, who read the rough manuscript and actually laughed: thank you. This inspired me to continue with the idea!

Introduction

There is no doubt that this question (Why did the Chicken Cross the Road?) has vexed many a scholar and ordinary person alike for longer than anyone cares to remember. Where does this obsession come from? Of all the jokes and quips of all time, what is so appealing and redeeming about such a simple one?

This project started with an e-mail passed around at a social function and by a few comments one day by friends on a road trip. We were all laughing so much and making jokes altering quotes to fit the chicken/road theme. We found them very funny and decided to start writing them down. It became an obsession that started me on a journey. The quest is not only to find the hidden meaning (if, in fact, there is one) behind this subtle but persistent riddle, but to find out what so many people could have said (given the opportunity) on the topic.

It seems that anybody and everybody, *whoever* they are, would have had an opinion on the most perplexing riddle of our time.

To understand how this icon of humor made its way into our hearts and lives, we need to go back in time and view some of the thoughts and words of our ancestors. It is from the great ones that we usually learn the greatest truths and insights.

Let's look at the Platonic view of this weighty question....."Good chickens do not need laws to tell them to act responsibly, while bad chickens will find a way around the laws."

Maybe Aristotelians would just answer "To actualize its potential." The list goes on.

It seems that almost everyone has had a viewpoint somewhere along the way. They are not all necessarily great minds or significant historical figures. They may be popular, notorious, famous, or just plain outspoken.

Some are profound, some are not, and some are just, well...you be the judge! Here's what they *might* have said.

Why Did the Chicken **_REALLY_** Cross the Road?

"Before enlightenment,
cross the road.
After enlightenment,
cross the road."

—Buddha

"Walk?! Hell, Scotty, we could BEAM the darn
thing across."

—Captain James T. Kirk

"To cross or not to cross,
that is the question."

—William Shakespeare

"Well, chicken, are *you* gonna do somethin'
or just stand there and bleed?"

—Wyatt Earp

Why Did the Chicken *REALLY* Cross the Road?

"The chicken lied to me. It could not possibly have crossed the road at that time. Do I have 'stupid' written on my forehead?"

—Judge Judy

"Off with its head!!!"

—Henry VIII

"Never interrupt a chicken when he is making a mistake."

—Napoleon Bonaparte

"It's obvious! There are fortunes to be made over there."

—Donald Trump

Why Did the Chicken **REALLY** Cross the Road?

"Ah know that when we are in arffice, our administration will provaad the funding, through stem cell research, that will make all chickens flar free above the road, and never again have to be killed and eaten."

—Senator John Edwards

"The chicken could cross tomorrow. But what if there is no tomorrow? There wasn't one today."

—Phil Connors *(Groundhog Day)*

Why Did the Chicken *REALLY* Cross the Road?

"I say to the chicken...
Never give up! Never surrender!"

—Jason Nesmith/Commander Taggart
(Galaxy Quest)

"If you can't get rid of the chicken in your closet,
you'd best teach it road sense."

—George Bernard Shaw

"Which came first, the chicken
or the road?"

—Homer (circa 700 B.C.)

Why Did the Chicken *REALLY* Cross the Road?

"To take a walk on the wild side."
—Lou Reed

"Isn't anyone concerned where
the chicken escaped from?"
—Clarence Anglin

"What was the question!? Why did the chicken...
what? You talkin' to me? You talkin' to me? You
talkin' to me? Then who the heck else are you
talkin' to? You talkin' to me? Well, I'm the only
one here. Who do you think you're talkin' to?
Oh, yeah? Huh? Ok."

—Travis Bickle *(Taxi Driver)*

Why Did the Chicken *REALLY* Cross the Road?

"Chicken? What's all this talk about
chicken? Why, I had an uncle who thought
he was a chicken. My aunt almost
divorced him, but we needed the eggs."

—Groucho Marx

"I'll get you, my pretty,
and your little chicky, too!"

—The Wicked Witch

"It's 106 miles to Chicago, we've got a full tank of gas, half a pack of cigarettes, it's dark, we're wearing sunglasses, and there's a chicken on the road. Hit it!"

—Elwood Blues *(Blues Brothers)*

Why Did the Chicken **_REALLY_** Cross the Road?

"I can already predict the outcome.
Would you like a leg or a breast?
    —Frances Stevens _(To Catch a Thief)_

"To go beyond the Yellow Brick Road."
    —Elton John

"CBS has just received documents
stating that chickens have been
secretly crossing roads for
years unbeknown to the American
public. We believe these documents
to be genuine and accurate. Stay
tuned while we investigate...."

—Dan Rather

9

Why Did the Chicken **REALLY** Cross the Road?

"Hell, I don't know man.
But I bet it had a better
childhood than me!"
—Eminem

"Life will find a way. Chickens are a form
of life, so they will find a way."
—John Hammond *(Jurassic Park)*

"They say Elvis is dead. I say, no, you're
looking at him. Elvis isn't dead; he just
changed into a chicken."
—Dennis Rodman

Why Did the Chicken **_REALLY_** Cross the Road?

"The chicken did what? The truth!
You want the truth? You can't HANDLE
the truth!"

—Colonel Nathan Jessep
(A Few Good Men)

"It chose to be daring; it chose to cross the road."

—J.F. Kennedy

Windows NT Chicken: Will cross
the road in June. No, August.
September for sure.

"I'm thinking .... I'm thinking."

—Jack Benny

Why Did the Chicken *REALLY* Cross the Road?

"Chickens are misled into believing there is a road by unscrupulous tire makers. Chickens aren't ignorant, but our society pays tire makers to create the need for these roads and then lures chickens into believing there is an advantage to crossing them. Down with roads; up with chickens."

—Ralph Nader

"May the road be with you."
—Obi-Wan Kenobi

"What! 'Chicken Crossing the Road'...Not without a fine white wine and a cup of heavy cream."
—Mario Batali

Why Did the Chicken **REALLY** Cross the Road?

"Cross the road you say? But how can you be sure? No one else would have known the chicken crossed the road except for the real killer!"

—Perry Mason

"It crossed becau ... Same to you, fella!"

—Bob Newhart

"To get to the Far Side."

—Gary Larsen

Why Did the Chicken **REALLY** Cross the Road?

"Why? Because it feels the need ...
the need for speed!"

—Lieutenant Pete 'Maverick' Mitchell
(Top Gun)

"Ay carumba!
Don't have a chicken, man!"

—Bart Simpson

"Why did the chi...let me answer this folks. The chick....let me tell you, the libs, yes, the liberals folks, caused....the...the question is...what was the question? Oh yeah, the chick...why don't people get this. How many times do I need to...."

—Rush Limbaugh

Why Did the Chicken *REALLY* Cross the Road?

"What's on the other side? Frankly,
my dear chicken, I don't give a damn."
—Rhett Butler

"As *my* pappy used to say, 'If someone
wants to bet you that that chicken
will cross the road to lay an egg,
warm up the skillet to make an omelet'."
—Brett Maverick

"There's only one attitude the
chicken should have. Enjoy the
ride while you're on it."
—Johnny Depp

Why Did the Chicken **REALLY** Cross the Road?

"Are you stupid??!! Didn't you see the chicken cross the line? I don't believe this!!"

—John McEnroe

Why Did the Chicken *REALLY* Cross the Road?

OS/2 Chicken: It crossed the road in style years ago, but it was so quiet that nobody noticed.

"The chickens just wanna go the distance."
—Rocky Balboa

"Cross! Cross! Cross! If I hear one more word about crossing the road, I'll run in the house and slam the door!"

—Scarlett O'Hara

"It is our road, and if we choose to blow it up, we don't care if the chicken is crossing."

**—Francois Mitterand
(Ex-French President)**

Windows 98 Chicken: It's got stronger legs, but it still falls over half way across the road.

"Right now I'm having amnesia and deja vu at the same time. I think I've forgotten why it crossed the road before."

—Steven Wright

"Why does anyone cross a road? I mean, why doesn't anyone ever think to ask, 'What the heck was this chicken doing walking all over the place anyway?'"

—Jerry Seinfeld

"The chicken not only failed to cross, it is no more. It has ceased to function. Bereft of life, it rests in peace. It's a stiff. If it wasn't nailed to the road it'd be pushing up daisies. It's snuffed it. Its metabolic processes are now history. It's bleeding demised. It's rung down the curtain, shuffled off the mortal coil and joined the bleeding Choir Invisible. This is an ex-chicken."

—John Cleese *(Monty Python)*

"If a chicken does its best to cross the road, what else is there?"

—General George Patton

"And now... page two... A chicken... attempts to cross... the street... yes... the street... and is... run down by a... Buick! The Buick Roadmaster with its powerful performance and elegant style! Yes... that poor chicken... hit by the Buick... it's true... It's... true... if it only took Citri-Cal, maybe it would have been saved, and speaking of true... visit your local True Value Hardware Store. And now....you know the <u>REST</u> of the story."

—Paul Harvey

Why Did the Chicken *REALLY* Cross the Road?

"Well. The chicken. Crossed the road. Or so we all thought. It now seems that the whole story. May have been invented. To boost. Interest in a new book published, published I might add yes, I might, I might, indeed published by the very same chook. Tonight on Holmes. We investigate. The chook book crook, ahmph."

—Paul Holmes

Windows ME Chicken:
Its parents disowned this chicken, so if it was hit by a car and buried, there would be much rejoicing.

Why Did the Chicken *REALLY* Cross the Road?

"Now even chickens can call for their free 10-minute reading. Your sign is coming into the 3rd house of Peterbuilt, I see you crossing a path of some sort, there are lines on the path... umm... your lucky number is 14 (click!)."

—Dionne Warwick

"Just did it."
—Nike Company

"And now, here's a hot new number from a hot young band whose drummer was so tragically killed in a freeway accident, it's The Hen House Flock singing 'When You Gonna Crow?', hitting the charts at number 23!"

—Casey Kasem

Why Did the Chicken *REALLY* Cross the Road?

"Did your hear about that chicken crossing the road last night? I mean, what is it with chickens these days? Roads are dangerous, y'know, tons of metal and rubber and all that, and chickens are small fluffy birds....I dunno, what do you think, maybe it's just me."

—Jay Leno

"Do, or do not. There is no 'try'."

—Yoda *(The Empire Strikes Back)*

"If they cross, we will fight them on the beaches."

—Winston Churchill

Why Did the Chicken *REALLY* Cross the Road?

"I invited it to come up and see me sometime."

—Mae West

Why Did the Chicken **_REALLY_** Cross the Road?

Windows 2000 Chicken: It crosses and crosses and crosses and crosses...

"I don't know why the chicken is there, but I'm pretty sure that it is not in order to enjoy itself."
—Ludwig Wittgenstein

"World domination. The same old dream. Our asylums are full of chickens who think they're Napoleon. Or God."
—James Bond

Why Did the Chicken *REALLY* Cross the Road?

"Warning! warning! warning!"
—The Robot *(Lost in Space)*

Windows XP Chicken: It crosses, identifies the models of car that are on the road, installs software that tells the driver that there is a 4lb. chicken on the road and instructs the car's onboard computer to take evasive action.

Macintosh Chicken: No reasonable chicken owner would want a chicken to cross the road, so there's no way to tell it to.

"It didn't. The rotation of the earth made it appear to cross."

—Jean Focault

"Because of those darn bleeding-heart liberals, trying to save one stupid bird while thousands of jobs are being lost..."

—Rush Limbaugh

27

Why Did the Chicken *REALLY* Cross the Road?

"Now the chicken goes along the dark road whence they say no one returns."

—Catullus (87–54? B.C.)

"To keep up with CURRENT events."

—Andre Ampere

"I am just so touched that a chicken would go to the trouble to dress up as a ghostly fry-cook and stand on the other side of the street just to entertain me. It must really like me!"

—Sponge Bob

Why Did the Chicken *REALLY* Cross the Road?

"She RESISTED the idea at first."

—Georg Ohm

"Hen Party 42%; Dare 18%;
Whim 12%; Business 2%;
Undecided 26%."

—George Gallup

"One night waits all;
Death's road we must all go,
even innocent chickens."

—Horace (65–8 B.C.)

Why Did the Chicken **REALLY** Cross the Road?

"The chicken will invariably cross the road at the worst possible time and the worst possible place."

—Section 41A, Murphy's Law

Microsoft™ Chicken: It's already on both sides of the road. And it just bought the road.

"Good Lord. A chicken crossing a road. Why, that's just plain stupid. It's just gonna git itself run over. Who in their right mind would let their chickens get out of the pen and allow them to wander all over the place? Don't they know the price of eggs or something?"

—The Fruitcake Lady

Why Did the Chicken *REALLY* Cross the Road?

"If you ask this question, you deny your own chicken nature."

—Buddha

"Chickens are an excellent source of protein. Their place is on a menu, not on a road."

—Pavarotti

"I have just released the new Chicken 2005, which will both cross roads AND balance your checkbook, although dividing 3 by 2 will get you 1.4999999999."

—Bill Gates

Why Did the Chicken *REALLY* Cross the Road?

"There are three truths in life. Hockey is a sport for white men and basketball is a sport for black men. Golf is a sport for white men dressed like black pimps. A chicken crossing the road is about as safe as a white golfer in Harlem."

—Tiger Woods

Why Did the Chicken *REALLY* Cross the Road?

"I'm ready. I'm ready. I'm ready. I'm ready. What's the question?"

—Sponge Bob

"Keep working hard and the chicken can get anything that it wants. If God gave it the talent, it should go for it. But don't think it's going to be easy. It's hard!"

—Aaliyah

"The chicken, knowing of its phobia, decided that crossing the road was the only way to a cure."

—Sigmund Freud

Why Did the Chicken **REALLY** Cross the Road?

"Ask not what the road can do for the chicken, but what the chicken can do for the road."

—J.F. Kennedy

"What do you take me for, an idiot?"

**—General Charles de Gaulle
(when a journalist asked him if he thought
the chicken would make it across)**

"My mama says that chickens are ornery because they got no teeth to bite or chew anything with. So I figure they are crossing the road to find out where to get some teeth."

—Bobby Boucher *(The Waterboy)*

Why Did the Chicken *REALLY* Cross the Road?

"We made it an offer it couldn't refuse."
—Vito Corleone

"Where there is one chicken, there will be more."
—George W. Bush

"In the end, everything is a gag. This is no exception."
—Charlie Chaplin

35

Why Did the Chicken **REALLY** Cross the Road?

"Three o'clock is always too late
or too early to cross."
—Jean-Paul Sartre

C Chicken: It crosses the road
without looking both ways.

"This is one small step for chicken,
but one giant leap for chickenkind."
—Neil Armstrong

"The glory of crossing is fleeting, but the obscurity
from never trying is forever."
—Napoleon Bonaparte

Why Did the Chicken *REALLY* Cross the Road?

"I have found the best way to give advice
to chickens is to find out what they want
and then advise them to do it."

—Harry S. Truman

C++ Chicken: The chicken wouldn't have to
cross the road; you'd simply refer to him
on the other side.

"You are a chicken of God;
you serve no purpose by
thinking small."

—Nelson Mandela

Why Did the Chicken **REALLY** Cross the Road?

"Don't stay on one side of the road, unless you can make money there."

—George Burns

"The only way to get rid of the temptation of crossing is to yield to it."

—Oscar Wilde

"The chicken that hesitates is a damned fool."

—Mae West

Why Did the Chicken **_REALLY_** Cross the Road?

"Victory goes to the chicken that
makes the next-to-last mistake."
**—Chessmaster Savielly
Grigorievitch Tartakower**

"The chicken should remember that to cross and
be elegant is to forget what one is wearing."
—Yves Saint Laurent

"Beginnings are scary.
Endings are usually sad.
But it's the middle of the
road that counts the most."
—Sandra Bullock

39

Why Did the Chicken *REALLY* Cross the Road?

"For fifteen minutes of fame."
—Andy Warhol

Why Did the Chicken *REALLY* Cross the Road?

"If you can't get rid of the chicken in your closet, you'd best teach it road sense."

—George Bernard Shaw

Java Chicken: If your road needs to be crossed by a chicken, the server will download one to the other side.

"It is not the chicken's road. It is the people's road!"

—Vladimir Lenin

41

Why Did the Chicken *REALLY* Cross the Road?

"A journey of a thousand miles begins with a single step. So does the journey across the road."

—Confucius

"Even if the chicken is on the right track, it'll get run over if it just sits there."

—Will Rogers

"A people that values its chickens above its principles soon loses both."

—Dwight D. Eisenhower

Why Did the Chicken *REALLY* Cross the Road?

"If you are going to cross the road
and pass through hell, keep going."
—Winston Churchill

"Some cause happiness wherever they cross;
others, whenever they cross."
—Oscar Wilde

"No matter what a chicken
looks like, if she's confident
and crosses the road
without caring, she's sexy."
—Paris Hilton

43

"The chicken did not fail. It just found 10,000 ways that wouldn't work."

—Thomas Edison

VB Chicken: USHighways!
TheRoad.cross (aChicken).

Why Did the Chicken **_REALLY_** Cross the Road?

"Life is pleasant. Death is peaceful. It's the crossing the road that's troublesome."

—Isaac Asimov

OOP Chicken: It doesn't need to cross the road, it just sends a message.

"If she's going to cross the road, appearance is something the chicken should definitely consider before going out."

—Usher

Why Did the Chicken **_REALLY_** Cross the Road?

"I'm sure the chicken had a wonderful time, but this wasn't it."

—Groucho Marx

"The chicken did not want to achieve immortality through crossing; it wanted to achieve immortality through not crossing."

—Woody Allen

"It was the experience of mystery – even if mixed with fear – that endangered chickens."

—Albert Einstein

Why Did the Chicken *REALLY* Cross the Road?

"Whenever they cross, they are followed
by a dog called 'Ego'."

—Friedrich Nietzsche

"Chicken history becomes more
and more a race between
education and catastrophe."

—H.G. Wells

Why Did the Chicken **REALLY** Cross the Road?

"The chickens are not retreating –
they are advancing in another direction."

—General Douglas MacArthur

Why Did the Chicken *REALLY* Cross the Road?

"We have art to save ourselves from the truth. Chickens, on the other hand, don't seem to care."

—Friedrich Nietzsche

"The mistakes are all waiting to be made."

—Chessmaster Savielly Grigorievitch Tartakower

"The graveyards are full of indispensable chickens."

—Charles de Gaulle

Why Did the Chicken **REALLY** Cross the Road?

"The chicken often regretted speaking of crossing, but never the silent action of doing so."

—Xenocrates (396–314 B.C.)

"Most chickens would sooner die than think; in fact, they do so."

—Bertrand Russell

Why Did the Chicken *REALLY* Cross the Road?

"Don't let it end like this. Tell them I said something."
—Last words of Pancho "Chicken" Villa

"It's kind of fun to see a chicken do the impossible."
—Walt Disney

"It's a strange thing, but when the chicken is dreading crossing the road and would give anything to slow down the traffic, it has a disobliging habit of speeding up."
—Harry Potter

Why Did the Chicken **REALLY** Cross the Road?

"Never trust a chicken that can think for itself if you can't see where it keeps its brain."

—Arthur Weasley
(Harry Potter and the Goblet of Fire)

"Chiefs! Our road is not built to last a thousand years, yet in a sense it is. When a road is once built, it is a strange thing how it collects traffic, how every year it goes on, more and more chickens are found to walk thereon, and others are raised up to repair and perpetuate it, and keep it alive."

—Robert Louis Stevenson

Why Did the Chicken **REALLY** Cross the Road?

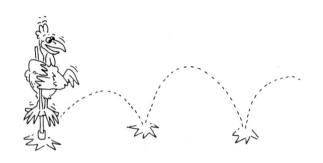

"While they are crossing, life speeds by."
—Seneca (3 B.C.–65.A.D.)

"If everything seems under control, it's just not crossing fast enough."
—Mario Andretti

Why Did the Chicken **_REALLY_** Cross the Road?

Delphi Chicken: The chicken is dragged across the road and dropped on the other side.

"If you want to make a chicken cross the road, you must first create the universe."
—Carl Sagan

"Quit now, you'll never make it.
If you disregard this advice,
you'll be halfway there."
—David Zucker

"The edges of this road are too far apart."
—Ambrose Bierce

"Cross and be damned, the chicken
can sleep when it's dead."
—Warren Zevon

"Everything has been figured out,
except how to cross."
—Jean-Paul Sartre

"There comes a time in the
affairs of a chicken when
she must take the bull by the
tale and face the situation."
—W.C. Fields

55

Why Did the Chicken **REALLY** Cross the Road?

"Because he can't get no.......satisfaction.... can't get no, oh no no no Hey hey hey, that's what I say."

—Mick Jagger

Why Did the Chicken *REALLY* Cross the Road?

"Never mistake the motion
of a chicken for action."
—Ernest Hemingway

"In any contest between the power and
the patience of a chicken, bet on patience."
—W.B. Prescott

"Not only is there no God,
but try finding a chicken on
a road on a Sunday."
—Woody Allen

"I'm sure the chicken crossed out of curiosity. Curiosity is not a sin....But we should exercise caution with our curiosity...yes, indeed."

—Albus Dumbldore
(Harry Potter and the Goblet of Fire)

"Crossing me, or the road, once is happenstance. Twice is coincidence. Three times is enemy action."

—Auric Goldfinger

"Obstacles cannot crush the chicken. Every obstacle yields to stern resolve. He who is fixed to a star does not change his mind."
—Leonardo da Vinci

"Be nice to chickens on your way across because you meet them on your way back."
—Jimmy Durante

"Chickens are not disturbed by things but the view they take of things."

—Epictetus (55–135 A.D.)

Gopher Chicken: Tried to run, but got flattened by the Web chicken.

"It is much more comfortable to be mad and know it, than to be a chicken and have one's doubts."

—G.B. Burgin

Why Did the Chicken **_REALLY_** Cross the Road?

"Argue for your limitations on your ability
to cross, and sure enough they're yours."
—Richard Bach

"If you gaze long at the other side,
the other side will gaze back at you."
—Friedrich Nietzsche

"Obstacles are those frightful
things you see when you take
your eyes off the road."
—Henry Ford

61

Why Did the Chicken *REALLY* Cross the Road?

Web Chicken: *Jumps out onto the road, turns right, and just keeps on running.*

"Success usually comes to those chickens that are too busy to be looking for it."
—Henry David Thoreau

"Chickens, like me, don't think about anything too much. They live in the present. They move on. They don't think about what happened yesterday. If they think too much, it kind of freaks them out."
—Pamela Anderson

Lotus Chicken: Don't you <u>dare</u> try to cross the road the same way we do!

"A pessimistic chicken sees the difficulty in every road; an optimistic one sees the opportunity in every difficulty."

—Winston Churchill

"For its part, the chicken travels, not to go anywhere, but to go. It travels for travel's sake. The great affair is to move!"

—Robert Louis Stevenson

63

Why Did the Chicken **REALLY** Cross the Road?

"Give us ten minutes with the chicken and we'll find out."

—L.A. Police Dept.

Why Did the Chicken **_REALLY_** Cross the Road?

"All the world's a stage and the chickens merely feathered players. They have their exits and their entrances, and one chicken in her time plays *many* parts."

—William Shakespeare

"If at first you don't succeed, try, try again. Then quit. *No* use being a *damn* fool about it."

—W.C. Fields

"This is the way the world ends for the chicken. Not with a bang but a cluck."

—T.S. Eliot

65

Why Did the Chicken **REALLY** Cross the Road?

"Open the pod bay doors, HAL. This chicken does not belong here."
"I'm sorry Dave, I'm afraid I can't do that."
—Dr. Dave Bowman / HAL *(2001: A Space Odyssey)*

"Dull, dull, dull!! Now if a peacock was crossing the road, that would get my attention!"

—Liberace

"If there's anything in the world I hate, it's chickens - filthy little devils!"
—Katherine Hepburn

Why Did the Chicken *REALLY* Cross the Road?

"You mean the chicken walk? Yeah I know, they gotta do it. It's a heredity thing that comes with the set, the neighborhood...when I was a kid I saw *my* big homies doin' it. It spread through the neighborhoods in '79, '78, somethin' like that."

—Snoop Dogg

"The activities of something that is served up on *my* plate on a regular basis really holds no interest for me."

—Genghis Khan

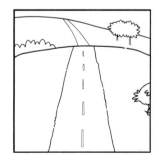

Why Did the Chicken *REALLY* Cross the Road?

Quantum Logic Chicken: The chicken is distributed probabalistically on all sides of the road until you observe it on the side of your course.

"This is typical! It takes a woman to take the first steps to do anything in this male-dominated society."

—Germain Greer

"Chickens inherently know they have but little time to live. Why not spend it being reckless?"

—Sterling Moss

"I believe that every chicken has the right to worship their God in their own way. Crossing the road is a spiritual journey and no chicken should be denied the right to cross the road in their own way."

—Senator Lieberman

Cray Chicken: Crosses faster than any other chicken, but if you don't dip it in liquid nitrogen first, it arrives on the other side fully cooked.

"Because it was there!"
—Sir Edmund Hillary

69

Why Did the Chicken **REALLY** Cross the Road?

"One chicken's fears are the good fortunes of others."
—W.C. Fields

"If you were building a road, which would you rather use? Two strong oxen or 1024 chickens?"
—Seymour Cray (father of supercomputing)

"It's always about the chicken! What about the poor drivers trying to avoid hitting the darn thing?"
—Jack Smith (Defensive Driving College)

"What will it find when it gets there? Happiness? Fulfillment? Food? Maybe just the desire to come back. Who really knows?"

—Lord Byron

"It's a waste of engineering, that's what it is. Roads were built for cars and trucks, not chickens. End of story."

—John Metcalf (19th-century road builder)

"It started out as an egg, for God's sake. Why shouldn't it aspire to greater things?"

—Madonna

71

Why Did the Chicken *REALLY* Cross the Road?

"The significant problems the chicken faced cannot be solved at the same level of thinking it was at when it created them."

—Albert Einstein

Why Did the Chicken *REALLY* Cross the Road?

"It must be great to be a chicken.
With low expectations it's very
easy to surprise people."

—Pamela Anderson

"A chicken can be destroyed but not defeated."

—Ernest Hemingway

"I'll tell you why only if you
get my name right. This really
bugs me! I go around saying
'Everyone repeat it with me:
Her-MY-oh-nee not Her-my-
WON or Her-my-OWN'."

—Emma Watson

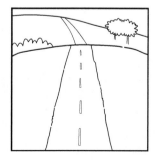

"The chicken may not have gone
where it intended to go, but I think it
ended up where it intended to be."
—Douglas Adams

"It has become appallingly obvious that our
chickens have exceeded our humanity."
—Albert Einstein

"The secret of crossing is knowing
more than other chickens."
—Aristotle Onassis

Why Did the Chicken *REALLY* Cross the Road?

"When you have to kill a chicken,
it costs nothing to be polite."
—Winston Churchill

"We all agree that the theory of a chicken
crossing a road is crazy, but is it crazy
enough?"

—Niels Bohr

"Show me a sane chicken
on a road and I will cure
him for you."

—Carl Jung

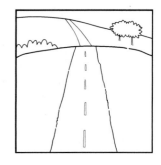

Why Did the Chicken **REALLY** Cross the Road?

"To die in the rain alone."

—Ernest Hemingway

"Basically, chickens no longer cross
for anything but the sensation
they have while crossing."

—Albert Giacometti

Why Did the Chicken **_REALLY_** Cross the Road?

"You know the world is going crazy when the best rapper is a white guy, the best golfer is a black guy, the tallest guy in the NBA is Chinese, the Swiss hold the America's Cup, France is accusing the U.S. of arrogance, Germany doesn't want to go to war. Why would you think a chicken crossing a road is strange?"

—Chris Rock

"First the chickens ignore you, then they laugh at you, then they fight you, then you win."

—Mahatma Gandhi

"Few things are harder to
put up with than a chicken
setting a good example."
—Mark Twain

"Whether the chicken thinks that he can cross,
or that he can't, he is usually right."
—Henry Ford

"Attention to crossing the road
is life's greatest hindrance."
—Plato (427-347 B.C.)

"There are some experiences in life which should not be demanded twice from any chicken, and one of them is listening to the Brahms Requiem."

—George Bernard Shaw

"There are only two tragedies in life: one is not getting to the other side, and the other is getting there."

—Oscar Wilde

Why Did the Chicken *REALLY* Cross the Road?

"You mighta got home this time chicken,
but it ain't over till it's over."

—Yogi Berra

Why Did the Chicken **REALLY** Cross the Road?

"If chickens didn't cross the road, all the money in the world would have no meaning."
—Aristotle Onassis

"My advice to you is to cross the road. If you find a rooster, you'll be happy; if not, you'll become a philosopher."
—Socrates (470–399 B.C.)

"The object of crossing the road is not to die for your country but to make the other chicken die for his."
—General George Patton

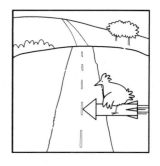

Why Did the Chicken **_REALLY_** Cross the Road?

"I missed one?"
—Colonel Sanders

"Why? Because the gods, too, are fond of a joke."
—Aristotle (384–322 B.C.)

"You can stop more chickens with a kind word and a gun than you can with a kind word alone."
—Al Capone

COBOL Chicken: 0001-CHICKEN-CROSSING.
IF NO-MORE-VEHICLES THEN
PERFORM
0010-CROSS-THE-ROAD
VARYING STEPS FROM 1 BY 1
UNTIL
ON-THE-OTHER-SIDE
ELSE
GO TO 0001-CHICKEN-CROSSING

"I am the chicken!!!!
  Ooh, somebody stop me!"
        —The Mask

Why Did the Chicken **REALLY** Cross the Road?

"I hate it when the title gives away the plot!"
—Dilbert

"'Cause it (bleeep)... wanted to.
That's the (bleeep)... reason."
—Jack Nicholson

"When I am working on a problem, I never think about the other side of the road. I only think about how to solve the problem. But when I have finished, if the solution is not arriving there, I know it is wrong."

—Buckminster Fuller

Why Did the Chicken **_REALLY_** Cross the Road?

"Lots of chickens want to ride with you in the limo, but what you want is a chicken that will take the bus with you when the limo breaks down."

—Oprah Winfrey

"There's nothing wrong with shooting chickens as long as the right chickens get shot."

—Clint Eastwood

"It didn't. I was playing golf with it at the time."

—O.J. Simpson

Why Did the Chicken **REALLY** Cross the Road?

"Not every chicken is meant to make a difference. But for most chickens, the choice to lead an ordinary life is no longer an option."

—Spiderman

"It's a darn poor chicken that can only think of one way to cross a road."

—Andrew Jackson, 7th U.S. President

"I forgot. I suffer from short term memory loss. It runs in my family...At least I think it does...What's a chicken anyway? I have never seen one or maybe I have? What was the question again."

—Dory _(Finding Nemo)_

Why Did the Chicken *REALLY* Cross the Road?

"In a world of pollution, profanity, adolescence, zits, broccoli, racism, ozone depletion, sexism, stupid guys, and PMS, why the heck do chickens think they can cross roads and get away with it?"
—Joanne Smith

"The chicken feels like an idiot. But it is an idiot, so it kinda works out."
—Billy Madison

"Be the chicken you want to see in the world."
—Mahatma Gandhi

"Go ahead, chicken, make my day."
—Harry Callahan (Dirty Harry)

"I am prepared to filibuster, if necessary, any Supreme Court nominee who would turn back the clock on a chicken's right to choose to cross the road..."

—Senator John Kerry

"What road?"

—Pyrrho the Skeptic

"Because that's the only kind of trip the 'Establishment' would let it take."

—Timothy Leary

89

Why Did the Chicken *REALLY* Cross the Road?

"Ain't no chicken can avoid being average, but ain't no chicken got to be common. Crossing the road is neither common nor average. It's just plain stupid."

—Satchel Paige

"Sometimes when you look in the chicken's eyes you get the feeling that someone else is driving."

—David Letterman

"Oh, like a bird on a wire, like a drunk in a midnight choir, the chicken has tried in its way to be free."

—Leonard Cohen

Why Did the Chicken **_REALLY_** Cross the Road?

"There's nothing like a nighttime stroll
across a road to give a chicken ideas."

—Mad-Eye Moody
(Harry Potter and the Goblet of Fire)

"If not crossing the road is like losing, the chicken
despises it, and would do anything to avoid it."

—Michael Jordan

"That chicken is too clumsy
and too slow to make it to
the other side."

—Branch Rickey

Why Did the Chicken **_REALLY_** Cross the Road?

"Chickens are big-time because they have wings. They could fly if they wanted to. Chickens don't want to cross the road. They don't need help crossing the road. In fact, I'm not interested in crossing the road myself."

—Dick Cheney

"To find a much better pic-a-nic."

—Yogi Bear

Why Did the Chicken *REALLY* Cross the Road?

"The chicken got in my way, and it was darn lucky it didn't have any ears!"
—Mike Tyson

"There's nothing worse than a sorry, pitiful, whining chicken when it loses or fails."
—Charles Barkley

"Fine art and pizza delivery: what chickens do on roads falls neatly in between."
—David Letterman

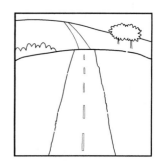

Why Did the Chicken **REALLY** Cross the Road?

"Chickens and people feel exactly the same fear. Chickens just react to it differently."

—Cus D'Amoto

"Once the chicken starts crossing, it can't change or pull up. It's all or nothing."

—Babe Ruth

"Smoking and cars kill. Chickens don't smoke but if they cross roads they can get killed. If you're killed, you've lost a very important part of your life."

—Brooke Shields

Why Did the Chicken **REALLY** Cross the Road?

"The road is just the beginning. I'm sure the chicken has greater plans that are just not being revealed to us right now."

—Tony Blair

"To challenge me for the Governorship of California, but it will be terminated!"

—Arnold Schwarzenegger

"As long as it doesn't compromise National Security, I frankly don't care where it's going or what its doing."

—Condoleezza Rice

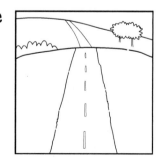

Why Did the Chicken **REALLY** Cross the Road?

"Fascinating, Captain. The chicken seems driven by a beam of pure energy."

—Mr. Spock

Why Did the Chicken **_REALLY_** Cross the Road?

"I oppose the actions of chickens, personally. I don't like chickens. I fought in Southeast Asia to prevent the invasion of chickens. I believe life does begin at conception, and this applies to chickens and their right to proliferate, or not. My view will never change on this subject, unless it does."

—Senator John Kerry

"Trying to sneak a fast ball past Hank Aaron is like trying to sneak a chicken past a rooster on a busy road."

—Curt Simmons

"The chicken needs to ask itself one big question : 'Am I in shape for this'?"

—Yogi Berra

"I don't know about you, but if I was cooped up like a chicken in those tiny, little cages and fed scraps, day in, day out, I'd be making a break for it, too."

—Kylie Minogue

Why Did the Chicken *REALLY* Cross the Road?

"Run and don't look back!!!!"
—Christopher Skase

"To boldly go where no chicken has gone before."
—Captain James T. Kirk

"It is a rough road that leads a chicken to the heights of greatness."
—Seneca (8 B.C.-65 A.D.)

"Yeah, but the problem is chickens are so preoccupied with whether or not they could cross, they didn't stop to think if they should."

—Dr. Ian Malcolm *(Jurassic Park)*

"Did you ever have the feeling that you wanted to go and still have the feeling that you wanted to stay? Well, chickens feel like this all the time."

—Banjo *(Man Who Came to Dinner)*

Why Did the Chicken **_REALLY_** Cross the Road?

"All chickens are seeking something they have lost. It is seldom that they find it and more seldom still that the attainment brings them greater happiness than the quest."

—Arthur C. Clarke

"Mmm, that dirty, double-crossin' chicken."

—James Cagney

"If the chickens hadn't done what I told 'em not to do, they'd still be alive today."

—Mr. Pink _(Reservoir Dogs)_

Why Did the Chicken **REALLY** Cross the Road?

"Did the chicken cross the road? Did it cross it with a toad? Yes! The chicken crossed the road, but why it crossed it, I've not been told!"

—Dr. Seuss

Why Did the Chicken **REALLY** Cross the Road?

"Nope, I don't know why it would want to do thaaat, but my Mama always says, 'stupid is as stupid does'."

—Forrest Gump

"Two roads diverged in a wood, and the chicken took the one less traveled by, and that has made all the difference."

—Robert Frost

"If you build it (the road), the chickens will come."

—Ray Kinsella

Why Did the Chicken **REALLY** Cross the Road?

"Crossing the road today is a race between civil engineers striving to build bigger and better super-highways, and the chicken trying to prove them bigger and better idiots. So far, the chicken is winning."

—Rich Cook

"They're not gonna catch the chicken. It's on a mission from God."

—Elwood Blues *(Blues Brothers)*

(teeth clenched) "You've got 24 hours to find out why that @!!*@!@ chicken crossed the road!!!"

—Walter Skinner

Why Did the Chicken *REALLY* Cross the Road?

"Roads? Where we're going we don't need
– roads. The chickens can have them."

—Doc *(Back to the Future)*

"How should I know?...
Maybe to be freakin'
rich and sexy like me."

—Britney Spears

105

Why Did the Chicken **REALLY** Cross the Road?

"It's just another headline catching stunt. Chickens are no different from people. They all crave fame and notoriety."

—Dan Rather

"It had a dream."

—Martin Luther King, Jr.

"Whether the chicken's crossing is fast or slow, the road is always the same."

—Chinese proverb

Why Did the Chicken *REALLY* Cross the Road?

"To me, a chicken is no different from us. I believe you make your day. You make your life. So much of it is all perception, and this is the form that I built for myself. I have to accept it and work within those compounds, and it's up to me. So it is with the chicken. It's gotta do what it feels is right to do.

—Brad Pitt

"I'm not so sure about chickens. If their IQ's were any lower they'd be geraniums."

—Russ Francis

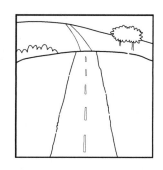

Why Did the Chicken **REALLY** Cross the Road?

"Character will only take the chicken so far. To get to the other side, it needs speed, timing, and above all, talent!"

—Karl Malone

Assembler Chicken: First it builds the road...

"Stay here on the outer limits of the dead-end zone? Nothing personal, but life at the end of the road just ain't for Captain Vic and his chicken. Sorry folks, but you can color us gone."

—Dan Ackroyd *(Neighbors)*

Why Did the Chicken **REALLY** Cross the Road?

"Do not try and stop the chicken. That's impossible. Instead, only try to realize the truth." ... "What truth?" ... "There is no chicken."

—Spoon Boy *(The Matrix)*

"To tiptoe through the tulips."

—Tiny Tim

"I'll find 'em for three but I'll catch 'em and kill 'em for ten ... Ten thousand bucks. For that you get the head, the feathers, the whole darn thing."

—Quint *(Jaws)*

109

Why Did the Chicken **REALLY** Cross the Road?

"The chicken didn't lose the game;
it just ran out of time."

—Vince Lombardi

Why Did the Chicken *REALLY* Cross the Road?

"If nothing else works, try prayer."
—Billy Graham

"A fish has an attention span of maybe 8 seconds. So, I reckon a chicken must have about 15. Is this long enough to get it to the other side?
—Stephen Hawking

"Think happy thoughts
and fly across the road."
—Peter Pan

"I have a really bad feeling about this."
—Han Solo

"I don't know why the chicken crossed the road, but I'll bet it was getting a government grant to cross the road, and I'll bet some leftist group out there is already forming a support group to help chickens with crossing-the-road syndrome. Can you believe this? How much more of this can real Americans take? Chickens crossing the road paid for by tax dollars, and when I say tax dollars, I'm talking 'bout your money, money the government took from you to build roads for chickens to cross."

—Rush Limbaugh

Why Did the Chicken *REALLY* Cross the Road?

"The great pleasure in any chicken's life is doing what people say can't be done."
—Henry David Thoreau

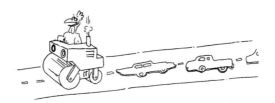

"Did you ever cross a road and forget why you went to the other side? I think that's how chickens spend their lives."

—Kirsten Dunst

Why Did the Chicken **_REALLY_** Cross the Road?

"I don't kill chickens that cross roads, but I like to mess with their minds. I hold them above buildings. They freak out and yell, 'Whoa, I'm way too high'!"

—Bruce Baum

"Damn the chicken! Save the Empire!"

—Ethan Randall

"Have you ever noticed? Anybody going slower than you is an idiot, and anyone going faster than you is a maniac. Chickens, on the other hand, don't seem to care."

—George Carlin

Why Did the Chicken *REALLY* Cross the Road?

"The chicken is thinking too small. The moon is the first milestone on the road to the stars."

—Arthur C. Clarke

"Is this chicken, what I have, or is this fish? I know it's tuna, but it says 'Chicken by the Sea'. Sorry, I wasn't listening. Why did what?"

—Jessica Simpson

"Is the chicken a taxpayer? If not, get it off the road to make way for taxpayers!"

—Walter Williams

Why Did the Chicken **REALLY** Cross the Road?

"Chickens have been driven
many times to their knees
by the overwhelming
conviction that they had
nowhere else to go."

—Abraham Lincoln

"It's so much fun acting, but I have this fear that
chickens are going to run away from me in terror
on the streets. They think I'm going to bite their
heads off or something."

—Lucy Liu

Why Did the Chicken **REALLY** Cross the Road?

"You see things like this; and you say 'Why?'
But then you dream things that never
were; and I say "Why not?"

—George Bernard Shaw

"How many chickens would have to cross before
they caused the equivalent damage of one car?
A heck of a lot, I would say. Let it cross! Let
them all cross! As often as they want to."

—John Muir

"Jesus said unto the chicken,
'With man this is impossible,
but with God all things are
possible'."

—Matthew 19:26

117

Why Did the Chicken **REALLY** Cross the Road?

"It is a journey fraught with danger. This is no insignificant undertaking for a chicken."

—Indiana Jones

Why Did the Chicken *REALLY* Cross the Road?

"Nobody gets to pick the time they die, but if you are a chicken on the edge of a road, intending to get to the other side, the odds are greatly improved."

—Jack Nicholson

"Just put one foot in front of the other and keep doing this until where you began is further away."

—Andy Griffith

"Never take your eye off the target. That way, if something tries to stop you, you won't see it until it's too late."

—Lee Harvey Oswald

119

Why Did the Chicken **REALLY** Cross the Road?

"The truth of the matter is that the chicken always knows the right thing to do. The hard part is doing it."

—General Norman Schwarzkopf

"Chickens can fly, you know. They just don't know how to think the right thoughts and levitate themselves off the ground."

—Michael Jackson

"You've got to ask yourself this question: 'What is motivating this chicken to do this'?"

—Tom Peters

Why Did the Chicken *REALLY* Cross the Road?

"You need to listen to the chicken
because the chicken is listening to *you*."

—Dr. Phil

"The chicken, like *me*, is a Mom, and it knows what
it has to do. It does not have a low self-esteem
problem or an inferiority complex, so don't even
question it. OK?!"

—Dr. Laura Schlessinger

"If I was a chicken and I was
asked if I would lay an egg
for *my* country, I'd do it."

—Bob Hope

Why Did the Chicken **REALLY** Cross the Road?

"Knowing the nature of roosters, I know darn well that it's gonna be followed."

—Sylvester Stallone

"Anybody who thinks the middle of the road is safe, hasn't stood in traffic for a long time."

—George Castanza

Why Did the Chicken *REALLY* Cross the Road?

"What were chickens doing before roads were built? Wandering around aimlessly?"

—Theodore Roosevelt

"If a chicken crosses a road and no one sees it, is it still a chicken?"

—Lao Tzu

"Forty-two."

—Douglas Adams

"Any chicken can cross a road when there is no danger."

—Publius Syrus

Why Did the Chicken **REALLY** Cross the Road?

"It probably crossed to get a better look at *my* legs, which, thank goodness, look good, dahling."

—Zsa Zsa Gabor

"It was a government conspiracy."

—Fox Mulder

"What's the difference between a chicken and a yogi? Nothing. They both want to get to the other side."

—Ted Theodosoff (Yoga teacher)

Why Did the Chicken *REALLY* Cross the Road?

"I fight for the chickens, and I am fighting for the chickens right now. I will not give up on the chickens crossing the road! I will fight for the chickens, and I will not disappoint them. Did I mention that I invented roads?"

—Vice-President Gore

"Because it'd made a mess of things over on this side of the road and figured it'd better get out right quick."

—John Constantine

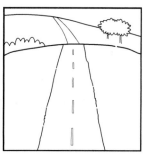

"To come, to see, to conquer."

—Julius Caesar

Why Did the Chicken **REALLY** Cross the Road?

"I've been waiting for you. We meet again, at last. The circle is now complete; when I left you, I was but the learner, now I am the master."

—Darth Vader (on the other side of the road)

Why Did the Chicken **REALLY** Cross the Road?

"I envision a world where all chickens will be free to cross roads without having their motives called into question."

—Martin Luther King, Jr.

"Because it would get across that road by any means necessary."

—Malcolm X

"For the greater good."

—Plato

Why Did the Chicken **REALLY** Cross the Road?

"The chicken did not cross the road. I repeat:
The chicken did not cross the road."

—Richard Nixon

"In order to act in good faith and be true
to itself, the chicken found it necessary to
cross the road."

—Jean-Paul Sartre

"And God came down from the heavens, and He
said unto the chicken, 'Thou shalt cross the road.'
And the Chicken crossed the road, and there was
much rejoicing."

—The Bible

Why Did the Chicken *REALLY* Cross the Road?

"Know ye that it is unclean to eat the chicken that has crossed the road and that the chicken that crosseth the road doth so for its own preservation?"

—Moses

"It probably fell from an airplane and couldn't stop its forward momentum."

—Gerald Ford

"Because of an excess of light pink gooey stuff in its pancreas."

—Hippocrates

Why Did the Chicken *REALLY* Cross the Road?

"I guess the worst that could happen
is that it could run a fowl of the law."

—N.Y. Police Dept.

"It was a historical
inevitability."

—Karl Marx

"I don't care. Catch it. Put it in prison. I need its
eggs to make my omelet – for the good of many
of course."

—Joseph Stalin

Why Did the Chicken *REALLY* Cross the Road?

"Forgive it Father, for it knows not what it does."

—Jesus Christ

"This was an unprovoked act of rebellion and we were quite justified in dropping 50 tons of nerve gas on it."

—Saddam Hussein

"Or was it the egg? We can never be sure. Or can we?"

—Bishop of Durham

131

Why Did the Chicken **REALLY** Cross the Road?

"One hundred percent pure adrenaline...
All the chicken's gotta do is jump."
—Bodhi *(Point Break)*

"Don't ever tell the chicken the odds!"
—Han Solo

"To earn a road-crossing Badge."
—Lord Baden-Powell

"To face a kinder, gentler thousand
points of headlights."
—George Bush, Sr.

"Build yourself a strong box;
fashion each part with care.
When it's strong as your
hand can make it, put all your
chickens there."

—Martha Stewart

"It was the logical next step
after coming down from
the trees."

—Charles Darwin

133

Why Did the Chicken **REALLY** Cross the Road?

"How many roads must one chicken cross?"
—Bob Dylan

Why Did the Chicken *REALLY* Cross the Road?

"There was no alternative."
—Margaret Thatcher

"To steal a job from a decent, hard-working American."
—Pat Buchanan

"National security was at stake."
—Oliver North

"I don't recall."
—Ronald Reagan

Why Did the Chicken **REALLY** Cross the Road?

"Whether the chicken crossed the road, or the road moved beneath the chicken, depends upon your point of view. The chicken did not cross the road. It transcended it."

—Albert Einstein

"Get busy crossing, or get busy dying."

**—Ellis Boyd "Red" Redding
(The Shawshank Redemption)**

Why Did the Chicken **_REALLY_** Cross the Road?

"It doesn't matter; the chicken's actions
have no meaning except to her."

—Albert Camus

"Chickens at rest tend to stay at rest.
Chickens in motion tend to cross the road."

—Sir Isaac Newton

"Where is he going?
To infinity, and beyond!"

—Buzz Lightyear

"It is the Mother of all Chickens."

—Saddam Hussein

Why Did the Chicken **REALLY** Cross the Road?

"What's the point of crossing a road
if nobody's watching?"

—Nicole Kidman

"In order to act in good faith and be true
to itself, the chicken found it necessary to
cross the road."

—Jean-Paul Sartre

"It was on the long and winding road...
that leads to your door..."

—Paul McCartney

Why Did the Chicken **_REALLY_** Cross the Road?

"Because it could not resist
the power of the Dark Side."
—Darth Vader

"The chicken, being an autonomous
being, chose to cross the road
of his own free will."
—Immanuel Kant

"Because it was the
road less traveled."
—M. Scott Peck

Why Did the Chicken **REALLY** Cross the Road?

"You saw it cross the road with your own eyes. How many more chickens have to cross the road before you believe it?"

—Fox Mulder

"It was a simple, bio-mechanical reflex that is commonly found in chickens."

—Scully

"If you saw me coming, you'd cross the road, too!"

—Mr. T

Why Did the Chicken *REALLY* Cross the Road?

"Strong and content the chicken
travels upon the open road."
—Walt Whitman

"Because it could not stop for death."
—Emily Dickinson

"The traffic started getting
rough; the chicken had to
cross. If not for the plumage
of its peerless tail the chicken
would be lost. The chicken
would be lost!"

—Gilligan

141

Why Did the Chicken *REALLY* Cross the Road?

"Get that freakin' chicken off the freakin' road or I'll break its freakin' neck!"

—New York cab driver

Why Did the Chicken **_REALLY_** Cross the Road?

"To live deliberately ... and suck
all the marrow out of life."
—Henry David Thoreau

"I believe that everything happens for a reason,
but I think it's important to seek out that reason.
That's how we learn."
—Drew Barrymore

"We're gonna catch the chicken,
give it a fair trial, followed by
a first-class hanging."
—Sheriff Cobb *(Silverado)*

Why Did the Chicken **REALLY** Cross the Road?

"I don't know. It's not that I'm lazy; it's that I just don't care."
—Peter Gibbons _(Office Space)_

Newton Chicken: Can't cluck, can't fly, and can't lay eggs, but you can carry it across the road in your pocket!

"I have a dream that one day all chickens will be judged, not by the color of their feathers, but by the content of their character."
—Martin Luther King, Jr.

Why Did the Chicken *REALLY* Cross the Road?

"Because it thought it could, it thought it could."
—The Little Engine that Could

"Hmmmmm... Chicken."
—Homer Simpson

"It didn't do it; nobody saw it do it. You can't prove anything."
—Bart Simpson

145

Why Did the Chicken **_REALLY_** Cross the Road?

"Gravity is the force that keeps the chicken on the road, but we have yet to discover which force moves it across."

—Sir Isaac Newton

"The chicken on the road should not become a constable of public opinion, but must dominate it. It must not become a servant of the masses, but their master!"

—Adolf Hitler

"Let us follow the chicken, hasten to retrace our steps and to regain the road, which alone leads to peace, liberty, and safety."

—Thomas Jefferson

Why Did the Chicken **_REALLY_** Cross the Road?

"Chickens, over great periods of time, have been naturally selected in such a way that they are now genetically dispositioned to cross roads."

—Charles Darwin

"I don't know why, but methinks I could rattle off a hundred-line soliloquy without much ado."

—William Shakespeare

"The news of its crossing has been greatly exaggerated."

—Mark Twain

Why Did the Chicken **REALLY** Cross the Road?

"Don't let this seemingly unimportant act fool you. Chickens are not as dumb as they look. There is a greater scheme afoot. Let us not sleep until we know what it is."

—General Erwin Rommel

"In the middle of difficulty, lies opportunity. In the middle of the road lies the chicken with an opportunity to face difficulty."

—Albert Einstein

Why Did the Chicken *REALLY* Cross the Road?

"Because the government had fooled him into thinking that he was crossing the road of his own free will, when he was really only serving their interests."

—George Orwell

"Show me the money, and I'll show you the chicken."

—Jerry Maguire

"And in the end the chicken winds up dyin' all alone on some dusty street. For what? For a tin star. It's all for nothin', Will. It's all for nothin'."

—Martin Howe *(High Noon)*

Why Did the Chicken **REALLY** Cross the Road?

"There are certain chickens that are marked for death. Like the ones that wander onto roads or those that treated me unfairly."

—Jennifer Lopez

"A chicken with such intent is mad, bad, and dangerous to know."

—Lady Caroline Lamb

"We are not sure which side of the road the chicken was on, but it was moving very fast."

—Werner Heisenberg

Why Did the Chicken *REALLY* Cross the Road?

"The question is not, 'Why did the chicken cross the road?' but rather, 'Who was crossing the road at the same time, whom we overlooked in our haste to observe the chicken crossing?'"

—Oliver Stone

"A chicken's got to know his limitations."

—Harry Callahan *(Dirty Harry)*

"What do I care? Did this Chicken commit any crime? 'Cause if it didn't, I've got way too many other things to worry about."

—Michael Garibaldi

151

"The chickens have come here to chew bubble gum and kick butt... and they're all out of bubble gum."

—John Nada *(They Live)*

"I believe in the incomprehensibility of God and of the actions of chickens."

—Honoré de Balzac

"Oops... Ack."

—Bill the Cat

Why Did the Chicken **REALLY** Cross the Road?

"The great question that has never been answered and which I have not been able to answer is... 'What does the chicken want?'"

—Sigmund Freud

"It didn't cross the road; it transcended it."

—Ralph Waldo Emerson

"Let the chicken not look back in anger or forward in fear, but around, in case something's coming."

—James Thurber

Why Did the Chicken **REALLY** Cross the Road?

"In my day, we didn't ask why the chicken crossed the road. Someone told us that the chicken had crossed the road, and that was good enough for us."

—Grandpa

"Once you eliminate the impossible odds of crossing, whatever remains, no matter how improbable, must be the truth."

—Sherlock Holmes

Why Did the Chicken **REALLY** Cross the Road?

"No. It's not going anywhere near a road! Now all you have to do is hold the chicken, bring me the toast, give me a check for the chicken salad sandwich, and you haven't broken any rules."

—Jack Nicholson

"The difference between 'involvement' and 'commitment' is like an eggs-and-ham breakfast: the chicken was 'involved', the pig must have been on the road."

—Grandma

Why Did the Chicken **REALLY** Cross the Road?

"Last night I shot a chicken crossing the street in *my* pajamas. How he got in *my* pajamas, I don't know."

—Groucho Marx

Why Did the Chicken *REALLY* Cross the Road?

"The instinct of nearly all societies is to lock up any chicken that is truly free. First, society begins by trying to eat you up. If this fails, they try to poison you. If this fails, too, they finish by loading honors on your head."

—Jean Cocteau

"Now I don't want to kill you chicken, and you don't wanna be dead, so I'd forget about crossing if I were you."

—Sheriff Cobb *(Silverado)*

157

Why Did the Chicken *REALLY* Cross the Road?

"The chickens were clearly confused as to where the dotted yellow line was leading. The only other option was to cross the line, so they did."

—South Florida voter

"The chicken is beginning to live a little, and feels less like a sick oyster at low tide."

—Louisa May Alcott

"Four score and seven years ago, our fathers brought forth on this continent, a new nation, conceived in Liberty, and dedicated to the proposition that all chickens are created equal."

—Abraham Lincoln

Why Did the Chicken **REALLY** Cross the Road?

'The chicken chose to cross the road. It chose to cross in this decade and do the other things, not because they are easy, but because they are hard. Because that goal will serve to organize and measure the best of its energies and skills, because that challenge is one that it was willing to accept, one it was unwilling to postpone, and one which it intends to win, and the others, too."

—John F. Kennedy

Why Did the Chicken **REALLY** Cross the Road?

"The chicken crossing the road is a clear statement to the world that drift netting and whale killing are longer acceptable. Soon ALL chickens will be on the other side of the road. Only then will we put a stop to this insanity."

—Paul Watson (Captain of *Sea Shepherd*)

"Death smiles at us all. All a chicken can do is smile back."

—Maximus Decimus Meridius *(Gladiator)*

Why Did the Chicken **_REALLY_** Cross the Road?

"Because 'tis better to suffer in
the mind the slings and arrows
of outrageous road maintenance
than to take arms against a sea
of oncoming vehicles..."

—Hamlet

"I don't believe we need to get
the chickens across the road.
I say, 'Give the road to the
chickens and let them decide'.
The government needs to let go
of strangling the chickens so
they can get across the road."

—George W. Bush

"Finally, you have broader considerations that might follow what you would call the 'Falling Chicken principle'. You have a row of chickens set up; you knock over the first one, and what will happen to the last one is the certainty that it will go over very quickly. So, you could have a beginning of a disintegration that would have the most profound influences."

—Dwight D. Eisenhower

"It wants to cross? I'll make it an offer it can't refuse."

—The Godfather

Why Did the Chicken **_REALLY_** Cross the Road?

Why?

...To go from the unreal to the real.

Write your quotes here and send them to us. For every quote we use in future editions, we will pay you! See our submissions page at www.jest-a-minute.com

Write your quotes here and send them to us. For every quote we use in future editions, we will pay you! See our submissions page at www.jest-a-minute.com

Write your quotes here and send them to us. For every quote we use in future editions, we will pay you! See our submissions page at www.jest-a-minute.com

Write your quotes here and send them to us. For every quote we use in future editions, we will pay you! See our submissions page at www.jest-a-minute.com

Write your quotes here and send them to us. For every quote we use in future editions, we will pay you! See our submissions page at www.jest-a-minute.com

Write your quotes here and send them to us. For every quote we use in future editions, we will pay you! See our submissions page at www.jest-a-minute.com

Write your quotes here and send them to us. For every quote
we use in future editions, we will pay you! See our submissions
page at www.jest-a-minute.com

Write your quotes here and send them to us. For every quote we use in future editions, we will pay you! See our submissions page at www.jest-a-minute.com

Index